PYTHON PROGRAMMING

PYTHON PROGRAMMING
THE STEP-BY-STEP
PYTHON CODING GUIDE

By Steven Giles

The trademarks that are used are without any consent, and the publication of the trademark is without permission or backing by the trademark owner. All trademarks and brands within this book are for clarifying purposes only and are the owned by the owners themselves, not affiliated with this document.

Disclaimer and Terms of Use: The Author and Publisher has strived to be as accurate and complete as possible in the creation of this book, notwithstanding the fact that he does not warrant or represent at any time that the contents within are accurate due to the rapidly changing nature of the Internet. While all attempts have been made to verify information provided in this publication, the Author and Publisher assumes no responsibility for errors, omissions, or contrary interpretation of the subject matter herein.

Any perceived slights of specific persons, peoples, or organizations are unintentional. In practical advice books, like anything else in life, there are no guarantees of results. Readers are cautioned to rely on their own judgment about their individual circumstances and act accordingly.

This book is not intended for use as a source of legal, medical, business, accounting or financial advice. All readers are advised to seek services of competent professionals in the legal, medical, business, accounting, and finance fields.

TABLE OF CONTENTS

INTRODUCTION

P ython, a high level language developed by Guido van Rossum, is known for its easy readability. The core philosophies of the language are simple - simplicity over complexity; beauty over ugliness, explicit over implicit and other similar aphorisms. The most important philosophy of the language is "Readability Counts", which means that the syntaxes and codes written using Python are clear and neat. The programming language has a huge library that supports programmers. Python also has an open source version called CPython programming platform. It has a huge community of developers who constantly work to upgrade features.

It has simple easy-to-use syntax, making it the perfect language for someone trying to learn computer programming for the first time.

Installing Python is generally easy, and nowadays many Linux and UNIX distributions include a recent Python. Even some Windows computers (notably those from HP) now come with Python already installed.

Python is a dynamic language and supports different programming styles including object-oriented, aspect-oriented, functional and imperative. One of the best features of the language is easy and enhanced memory management. Essentially employed as a scripting language, Python offers a great level of functionality. While it can be used as a standalone program, you can also integrate third party tools and customize its functionality.

One of the highlights of Python is that it is a highly extensible language. This means that various functional elements are not built into the core of this platform. Rather, you can use third party applications and extend the platform's functionality.

Additionally, you can also integrate a Python code into an existing program and create an interface for programming. This is called Embedding and Extending.

Like mentioned above, syntaxes of Python are simple. Complicated syntaxes are rejected and the platform embraces codes that are less cluttered and sparse. However, this does not in any way influence the performance or functionality of programs. Also, unlike other popular programming languages such as Perl, Python does not offer unnecessary clutter by giving the programmer multiple ways of achieving the same purpose. Python's philosophy is to offer one powerful way or obtaining one result. This philosophy is the main driving force behind the simplicity of Python. So, if you want to become adept in this language, you need to change your mindset and think in a simple and straightforward manner. This approach towards programming works best with Python.

In order to aid simplicity, Python coding and syntaxes use English words rather than punctuations or symbols. This enhances the readability as well. Some examples of statements written in Python include "if", "for", "while", "try", "class", "def", "with", "yield", "import" and many others. Most of the commands used are self explanatory.

Owing to the ease of handling, Python is a "programmer's language". Moreover, learning the language is very simple. One of the biggest advantages of Python, besides clear and easily readable codes, is the speed with which you can code. Programmers can go on fast track because multiple levels which are not necessary can be skipped. Another advantage is that programmers get a lot of support from the Python open source developer community.

The portability feature of Python is another one of its major strengths. Not only can Python run on multiple platforms, but also programmers only need to write a single program to work on all operating systems such as Linux, Mac, Windows and others. It is a highly adaptable language.

Learning Python is not a tough task even for beginners. So, take the leap and master the Python.

This is a comprehensive guide on how to get started in Python, why you should learn it and how you can learn it.

THE REASON BEHIND THE HUGE DEMAND OF PYTHON DEVELOPERS

Python is a gem in the IT industry: Python was conceived in early 1980s and presented to the industry in late 80s. Due to lack of proper marketing, it could not gather the notice of the industry for more than decades. Moreover, it has some inbuilt issues with the core concept and that has been working as an obstacle in its success path. In twenty first century, Google brought it from dirt and made some necessary changes over its set up and configurations. As a result, it gained the power and performance that it has within itself but in a secret nutshell come to the industry. Google modified the core logic of the language and it also deleted all the repeated modules and methods from the library making it lighter and smoother. Now, it increased its performance by twice or thrice. Hence it becomes one of the most powerful languages in the industry. In past decade, it has received tremendous popularity among the developers and tech experts and turned out as a gem in the IT industry.

Python developers can build efficient and powerful web applications: Due to its tremendous power and efficiency, a python developer can build enterprise standard high performance software applications in different domain. The tag line of Python is "Batteries included" means, all the required modules, methods and classes are there inside the language through different libraries. Well, due to presence of all these resources, the development process becomes much easier than before. Moreover, these inbuilt resources are highly optimized and hence can give the python developer better mileage. To add this, the resources are extremely compatible with other components of the language making it even powerful.

Python enables software developers building modern applications in different domains: Well, Python was heavily inspired from C++ and Java and hence we can expect many similar features within python as that in C++ or Java. Python has the capability to build any type of application just like Java i.e. a python developer can build desktop software, web application, hardware program or even smart phone games. This is really a terrific feature of python and it enables its developers not to limit their talent in any specific domain. They can develop any application irrespective of domain, device and platform.

Reliability and quality is at its par of excellence: Well, Python is famous for its efficiency, speed and reliability. You can project a Python application under any circumstance and you will get an amazing performance there. It is also extremely safe and secure. It has the potential in developing enterprise standard highly secure applications using 128 bit encryption technology. Moreover, you can also implement multi tier security measures in your application.

Availability of many supportive environments: Support matters a lot in IT industry. Fortunately, there is a huge community of Python developer's in the industry. Hence you can get instant online support from them during your difficulties. Moreover there are many python developers portal where you can resolve your doubt and confusion.

WHY LEARN THE PYTHON PROGRAMMING LANGUAGE? 9 FEATURES OF PYTHON

Python is a programming language developed by Guido van Rossum. It is a dynamically typed language with very high level data structures. It is used in a number of places including Google and Nasa.

FEATURES OF PYTHON.

1. DYNAMICALLY TYPED.

Variables do not have any type in the python programming language. You do not need to say

int x = 10

Instead you would write

x = 10

2. VERY HIGH LEVEL DATA STRUCTURES.

List, dictionary and sets are build in data types which allow very high levels of abstraction in a language like python.

3. SUPPORT FOR FUNCTIONAL PROGRAMMING.

Functions are firsts class objects which means they can be used like any other variable. This, with other functions like map, filter and reduce provides functional programming.

4. MULTI PARADIGM PROGRAMMING.

Python has support for multiple paradigms like object oriented programming, functional programming or iterative programming.

5. RAPID PROTOTYPING.

High level data structures along with dynamic typing make rapid prototyping a breeze in Python

6. BATTERIES INCLUDED.

Python believes in the philosophy of batteries included. This means that a large number of libraries are provided with python making programs written in python much shorter that in other languages.

7. SIGNIFICANT WHITESPACES.

Whitespaces are significant in the Python programming language. This makes code very easy to read in Python.

8. LIMITED NUMBER OF KEYWORDS.

The number of keywords in the python language are very limited. This makes it an easy language to learn for beginners. The core of the language is kept very small and functionalities are provided by other modules.

9. NAMESPACES.

Python tries to keep the namespace as keep as possible.

PYTHON KEYWORDS AND IDENTIFIER

PYTHON KEYWORDS

Keywords are the reserved words in Python.

We cannot use a keyword as variable name, function name or any other identifier. They are used to define the syntax and structure of the Python language.

In Python, keywords are case sensitive.

There are 33 keywords in Python 3.3. This number can vary slightly in course of time.

All the keywords except True, False and None are in lowercase and they must be written as it is. The list of all the keywords are given below.

Keywords in Python programming language

False	class	finally	is	return
None	continue	for	lambda	try
True	def	from	nonlocal	while
and	del	global	not	with
as	elif	or	yield	
assert	else	import	pass	
break	except	in	raise	

Looking at all the keywords at once and trying to figure out what they mean might be overwhelming.

If you want to have an overview, here is the complete list of all the keywords with examples.

PYTHON IDENTIFIERS

Identifier is the name given to entities like class, functions, variables etc. in Python. It helps differentiating one entity from another.

RULES FOR WRITING IDENTIFIERS

1. Identifiers can be a combination of letters in lowercase (a to z) or uppercase (A to Z) or digits (0 to 9) or an underscore (_). Names like myClass, var_1 and print_this_to_screen, all are valid example.

2. An identifier cannot start with a digit. 1variable is invalid, but variable1 is perfectly fine.

3. Keywords cannot be used as identifiers.

```
>>> global = 1
  File "<interactive input>", line 1
    global = 1
         ^
SyntaxError: invalid syntax
```

4. We cannot use special symbols like !, @, #, $, % etc. in our identifier.

```
>>> a@ = 0
  File "<interactive input>", line 1
    a@ = 0
       ^
SyntaxError: invalid syntax
```

5. We cannot use special symbols like !, @, #, $, % etc. in our identifier.

```
>>> a@ = 0
  File "<interactive input>", line 1
    a@ = 0
     ^
```

SyntaxError: invalid syntax

6. Identifier can be of any length.

THINGS TO CARE ABOUT

Python is a case-sensitive language. This means, Variable and variable are not the same. Always name identifiers that make sense.

While, c = 10 is valid. Writing count = 10 would make more sense and it would be easier to figure out what it does even when you look at your code after a long gap.

Multiple words can be separated using an underscore, this_is_a_long_variable.

We can also use camel-case style of writing, i.e., capitalize every first letter of the word except the initial word without any spaces. For example: camelCaseExample

WHAT ARE THE IMPORTANT REASONS TO LEARN THE PYTHON PROGRAMMING LANGUAGE?

Python is an open-source and high-level programming language developed for use with a broad range of operating systems. It is termed as most powerful programming language due to its dynamic and diversified nature. Python is easy-to-use with simple syntax and people who learn it for the first time find it very easy to grab the concepts. Having used by pioneer websites such as YouTube, Drop Box, Python has high demand in the market. If you would want to get the benefit of Python, register to Python Training.

Let's now learn the important reasons due to which Python language is used at a wider range of people.

* OBJECT ORIENTED PROGRAMMING

One of the powerful tools of Python is Object Oriented Programming, which allows data structures creation and reusability. Due to this reusability, the work is done efficiently and reduces a lot of time. During recent years, object oriented programming pertains to classes and many interactive objects. Object Oriented Programming techniques can be used in any of the software and can be implemented in any of the programming languages.

* READABILITY

With the simple syntax, the python coding language is very easy to understand. Hence, Python can be used as a prototype and can be implemented in other programming language after testing the code.

* PYTHON IS FREE

As Python is an open-source programming language, it is free of cost and allow unrestricted use. With this open-source license, it can be modified, redistributed and used commercially. The license is available even for entire source code with cost free support. CPython, the most widely used implementation of Python, can be used in all operating systems. Being the well designed, robust software with scalable and portable capabilities has become a widely used programming language.

* PROGRAMMING AT A FASTER RATE

Python is a high-level language and when programming using this language is quite faster when compared to the execution time done using the other low level languages.

* CROSS-PLATFORM OPERATING ABILITY

Python can be executed on all the major operating systems such as Mac OS, Microsoft Windows, Linus, and Unix. This programming language gives the best experience to work with any of the OS.

INTEGRATION CAPABILITIES

Following are the notable integration capabilities of Python:

- Process control capabilities are powerful

- Ability to be embedded as scripting programming language

- Easy to develop web services

- Helps to implement many internet protocols

If you interested to work with Python, register into one of the Python Training Institute where the candidates get more benefits out of the training. For information see, Python Training. Highly talented and professional faculties take the training sessions for the aspirants get a good understanding. Aspirants can check their understanding level with the help of the mock tests available online. Accurate test results will be given in the form of analytical reports. The aspirants can also opt for the other learning solutions such as corporate training, Boot camp training, classroom training etc.

WHY PYTHON HAS BECOME AN INDUSTRY FAVORITE AMONG PROGRAMMERS

With the world stepping towards a new age of technology development, it isn't hard to imagine a future that will be full of screens. And if so be the case then, demand for people with strong programming skills will definitely rise with more number of people required to develop and support the applications. Python Training is always a good idea for those wishes to be a part of this constantly developing industry. Python language is not only easy to grasp, but emphasizes less on syntax which is why a few mistakes here and there doesn't give as much trouble as some other languages does.

WHAT MAKES PYTHON A PREFERRED CHOICE AMONG PROGRAMMERS?

Python happens to be an easy programming language which offers its support to various application types starting from education to scientific computing to web development. Tech giants like Google along with Instagram have also made use of Python and its popularity continues to rise. Discussed below are some of the advantages offered by Python:

FIRST STEPS IN THE WORLD OF PROGRAMMING

Aspiring programmers can use Python to enter the programming world. Like several other programming languages such as Ruby, Perl, JavaScript, C#, C++, etc. Python is also object oriented based programming language. People who have thorough knowledge of Python can easily adapt to other environments. It is always recommended to acquire working knowledge so as to become aware of the methodologies that are used across different applications.

SIMPLE AND EASY TO UNDERSTAND AND CODE

Many people will agree to the fact that, learning and understanding a programming language isn't that exciting as compared to a tense baseball game. But, Python on the other hand was specifically developed keeping in mind newcomers. Even to the eye of a layman, it will seem meaningful and easy to understand. Curly brackets and tiring variable declarations are not part of this programming language thus, making it a lot easier to learn language.

GETTING INNOVATIVE

Python has helped in bringing real world and computing a lot close with it Raspberry Pi. This inexpensive, card-sized microcomputer helps tech enthusiasts to build various DIY stuffs like video gaming consoles, remote controlled cars and robots. Python happens to be the programming language that powers this microcomputer. Aspirants can select from different DIY projects available online and enhance their skills and motivations by completing such projects.

PYTHON ALSO SUPPORTS WEB DEVELOPMENT

With its huge capabilities, Python is also a favorite among web developers to build various types of web applications. The web application framework, Django has been developed using Python and serves as the foundation for popular websites like 'The Guardian', 'The NY Times', 'Pinterest' and more.

PYTHON STATEMENT, INDENTATION AND COMMENTS

In this part of the eBook, you will learn about Python statements, why indentation is important and use of comments in programming.

PYTHON STATEMENT

Instructions that a Python interpreter can execute are called statements. For example, a = 1 is an assignment statement. if statement, for statement, while statement etc. are other kinds of statements which will be discussed later.

MULTI-LINE STATEMENT

In Python, end of a statement is marked by a newline character. But we can make a statement extend over multiple lines with the line continuation character (\ ). For example:

```
a = 1 + 2 + 3 + \
    4 + 5 + 6 + \
    7 + 8 + 9
```

This is explicit line continuation. In Python, line continuation is implied inside parentheses ( ), brackets [ ] and braces { }. For instance, we can implement the above multi-line statement as

```
a = (1 + 2 + 3 +
    4 + 5 + 6 +
    7 + 8 + 9)
```

Here, the surrounding parentheses ( ) do the line continuation implicitly. Same is the case with [ ] and { }. For example:

```
colors = ['red',
          'blue',
          'green']
```

We could also put multiple statements in a single line using semicolons, as follows

```
a = 1; b = 2; c = 3
```

PYTHON INDENTATION

Most of the programming languages like C, C++, Java use braces { } to define a block of code. Python uses indentation.

A code block (body of a function, loop etc.) starts with indentation and ends with the first unindented line. The amount of indentation is up to you, but it must be consistent throughout that block.

The enforcement of indentation in Python makes the code look neat and clean. This results into Python programs that look similar and consistent.

Indentation can be ignored in line continuation. But it's a good idea to always indent. It makes the code more readable. For example:

```
if True:
    print('Hello')
    a = 5
```

and

```
if True: print('Hello'); a = 5
```

both are valid and do the same thing. But the former style is clearer.

Incorrect indentation will result into IndentationError.

PYTHON COMMENTS

Comments are very important while writing a program. It describes what's going on inside a program so that a person looking at the source code does not have a hard time figuring it out. You might forget the key details of the program you just wrote in a month's time. So taking time to explain these concepts in form of comments is always fruitful.

In Python, we use the hash (#) symbol to start writing a comment.

It extends up to the newline character. Comments are for programmers for better understanding of a program. Python Interpreter ignores comment.

```
#This is a comment
#print out Hello
print('Hello')
```

MULTI-LINE COMMENTS

If we have comments that extend multiple lines, one way of doing it is to use hash (#) in the beginning of each line. For example:

```
#This is a long comment
#and it extends
#to multiple lines
```

Another way of doing this is to use triple quotes, either ''' or """.

These triple quotes are generally used for multi-line strings. But they can be used as multi-line comment as well. Unless they are not docstrings, they do not generate any extra code.

"""This is also a
perfect example of
multi-line comments"""

DOCSTRING IN PYTHON

Docstring is short for documentation string.

It is a string that occurs as the first statement in a module, function, class, or method definition. We must write what a function/class does in the docstring.

Docstring is available to us as the attribute __doc__ of the function. Issue the following code in shell once you run the above program.

```
>>> print(double.__doc__)
Function to double the value
```

HOW TO INSTALL AND RUN PYTHON IN MAC OS X

1. Go to Download Python page on the official site and click Download Python 3.5.2 (You may see different version name).

2. When the download is complete, open the package and follow the instructions. You will see "The installation was successful" message when Python is successfully installed.

3. It's recommended to download a good text editor before you get started. If you are a beginner, I suggest you to download Sublime Text. It's free.

4. The installation process is straight forward. Run the Sublime Text Disk Image file you downloaded and follow the instructions.

5. Open Sublime Text and go to File > New File (Shortcut: Cmd+N). Then, save (Cmd+S or File > Save) the file with .py extension like: hello.py or first-program.py

6. Write the code and save it again. For starters, you can copy the code below:

   print "Hello, World!"
   This simple program outputs "Hello, World!"

7. Go to Tool > Build (Shortcut: Cmd + B). You will see the output at the bottom of Sublime Text.Congratulations, you've successfully run your first Python program.

HOW TO INSTALL AND RUN PYTHON IN LINUX (UBUNTU)

1. Install the following dependencies:

   $ sudo apt-get install build-essential checkinstall
   $ sudo apt-get install libreadline-gplv2-dev libncursesw5-dev libssl-dev libsqlite3-dev tk-dev libgdbm-dev libc6-dev libbz2-dev

2. Go to Download Python page on the official site and click Download Python 3.5.2 (You may see different version name).

3. In the terminal, go to the directory where the file is downloaded and run the command:

   $ tar -xvf Python-3.5.2.tgz
   This will extract your zipped file. Note: The filename will be different if you've downloaded a different version. Use the appropriate filename.

4. Go to the extracted directory.

   $ cd Python-3.5.2

5. Issue the following commands to compile Python source code on your Operating system.

   $ ./configure
   $ make
   $ make install

6. We recommend you to install Sublime Text if you are a newbie. To install Sublime Text in Ubuntu (on 14.04). Issue following commands.

```
sudo add-apt-repository -y ppa:webupd8team/sublime-text-2
sudo apt-get update
sudo apt-get install sublime-text
```

7. Open Sublime text. To create a new file, go to File > New File (Shortcut: Ctrl+N).

8. Save the file with .py file extension like: hello.py or first-program.py

9. Write the code and save it (Ctrl+S or File > Save) . For starters, you can copy the code below:

    print "Hello, World!"
    This simple program outputs "Hello, World!"

10. Go to Tool > Build (Shortcut: Ctrl+B). You will see the output at the bottom of Sublime Text. Congratulations, you've successfully run your first Python program.

HOW TO INSTALL AND RUN PYTHON IN WINDOWS

1. Go to Download Python page on the official site and click Download Python 3.5.2 (You may see different version name).

2. When the download is completed, double-click the file and follow the instructions to install it.

    When Python is installed, a program called IDLE is also installed along with it. It provides graphical user interface to work with Python.

3. Open IDLE, copy the following code below and press enter.

    print "Hello, World!"

4. To create a file in IDLE, go to File > New Window (Shortcut: Ctrl+N).

5. Write Python code (you can copy the code below to display sum of two numbers) and save (Shortcut: Ctrl+S) with .py file extension like: hello. py or your-first-program.py

    ```
            # add two numbers
    a = 5
    b = 6
    sum = a + b
    print(sum)
    ```

6. Go to Run > Run module (Shortcut: F5) and you can see the output. Congratulations, you've successfully run your first Python program.

ROLE OF PYTHON IN IMAGE APPLICATIONS

I n this part of the ebook we are going to know how Python plays an important role in image applications. Python is a high level programming language that lets you work more quickly and integrate your systems more effectively. 90% of people prefer Python over other technology because of its simplicity, reliability and easy interfacing. It is often compared to Lisp, Tcl, Perl, Ruby, C#, Visual Basic, Visual Fox Pro, Scheme or Java. It can be easily interfaced with C/ObjC/ Java/Fortran. It runs on all major operating systems such as Windows, Linux/ Unix, OS/2, Mac, Amiga, etc. Day by day we can see a rapid growth in Python Development.

Python supports multiple programming paradigms and modules. Python is also supported for the Internet Communications Engine (ICE) and many other integration technologies. It is packed with rich libraries and many add-on packages to tackle specific tasks. Python is friendly language you can learn it easily. Python used in many business, government, non-profit organizations, Google search engine, YouTube, NASA, the New York Stock Exchange, etc. Python is often used as a scripting language, but is also used in a wide range of non-scripting contexts. It provides very clear and readable syntax. You can easily write programs using this language. The Python code runs more than fast enough for most applications. It is used in a wide variety of application domains. Python is an excellent language for learning object orientation.

APPLICATIONS WRITTEN IN PYTHON ARE

- Web Applications (Django, Pylons)

- Games (Eve Online - MMORPG).

- 3D CAD/CAM.

- Image Applications.

- Science and Education Applications.

- Software Development (Trac for Project Management).

- Object Databases (ZODB / Durus).

- Network Programming (Bittorent).

- Mobile applications.

- Audio/Video Applications.

- Office Applications.

- Console Applications.

- Enterprise Applications.

- File Formats.

- Internet Applications.

- Python in Image Applications

Always images play a big role in reaching the audience than the words in the web application field. Because a picture is worth a thousand words. Generally some users can satisfy with the existing images but some users want to make some creativity or changes to an image. In order to fulfil their demands Python provides various programs. Let's see how Python used in imaging applications

- Gnofract 4D is a flexible fractal generation program, allows user to create beautiful images called fractals. Based on mathematical principles, the computer created the images automatically, include the Mandelbrot and Julia sets and many more. It doesn't mean that you need to do math for creating the images. Instead you can use your mouse to create more images as per your wish. Basically it runs on Unix-based systems such as Linux and

- FreeBSD and can also be run on Mac OS X. It is very easy to use, very fast, and flexible with an unlimited number of fractal functions and vast amount of options. It is a widely used open source program.

- Gogh is a PyGTK-based painting program or image editor with support for pressure-sensitive tablets/devices.

- ImgSeek is a photo collection manager and viewer with content-based search. It has many features. If you want to find a particular item, you simply sketch the image or you can use another image in your collection. It provides you with what you exactly need.

- VPython is the Python programming language plus a 3D graphics module called "visual". By using it you can easily create objects in 3D space and animations etc. It helps you to display the objects in a window. VPython allows the programmers to focus more on the computational aspect of their programs.

- MayaVi is a scientific visualization program based on the Visualization Toolkit (VTK), supports volume visualization of data via texture and ray cast mappers. It is easy to use. It can be imported as a Python module from other Python programs and can also be scripted from the Python interpreter.

PYTHON VARIABLES AND DATA TYPES

In this part, you will learn about variables, rules for naming a variable and different types of variable you can create in Python.

PYTHON VARIABLES

A variable is a location in memory used to store some data (value).

They are given unique names to differentiate between different memory locations. The rules for writing a variable name is same as the rules for writing identifiers in Python.

We don't need to declare a variable before using it. In Python, we simply assign a value to a variable and it will exist. We don't even have to declare the type of the variable. This is handled internally according to the type of value we assign to the variable.

VARIABLE ASSIGNMENT

We use the assignment operator (=) to assign values to a variable. Any type of value can be assigned to any valid variable.

a = 5
b = 3.2
c = "Hello"

Here, we have three assignment statements. 5 is an integer assigned to the variable a.

Similarly, 3.2 is a floating point number and "Hello" is a string (sequence of characters) assigned to the variables b and c respectively.

MULTIPLE ASSIGNMENTS

In Python, multiple assignments can be made in a single statement as follows:

a, b, c = 5, 3.2, "Hello"
If we want to assign the same value to multiple variables at once, we can do this as

x = y = z = "same"
This assigns the "same" string to all the three variables.

DATA TYPES IN PYTHON

Every value in Python has a datatype. Since everything is an object in Python programming, data types are actually classes and variables are instance (object) of these classes.

There are various data types in Python. Some of the important types are listed below.

PYTHON NUMBERS

Integers, floating point numbers and complex numbers falls under Python numbers category. They are defined as int, float and complex class in Python.

We can use the type() function to know which class a variable or a value belongs to and the isinstance() function to check if an object belongs to a particular class.

Integers can be of any length, it is only limited by the memory available.

A floating point number is accurate up to 15 decimal places. Integer and floating points are separated by decimal points. 1 is integer, 1.0 is floating point number.

Complex numbers are written in the form, x + yj, where x is the real part and y is the imaginary part. Here are some examples.

```
>>> a = 1234567890123456789
>>> a
1234567890123456789
>>> b = 0.1234567890123456789
>>> b
0.12345678901234568
>>> c = 1+2j
>>> c
(1+2j)
```

Notice that the float variable b got truncated.

PYTHON LIST

List is an ordered sequence of items. It is one of the most used datatype in Python and is very flexible. All the items in a list do not need to be of the same type.

Declaring a list is pretty straight forward. Items separated by commas are enclosed within brackets [ ].

```
>>> a = [1, 2.2, 'python']
```

We can use the slicing operator [ ] to extract an item or a range of items from a list. Index starts form 0 in Python.

Lists are mutable, meaning, value of elements of a list can be altered.

```
>>> a = [1,2,3]
>>> a[2]=4
>>> a
[1, 2, 4]
```

PYTHON TUPLE

Tuple is an ordered sequence of items same as list.The only difference is that tuples are immutable. Tuples once created cannot be modified.

Tuples are used to write-protect data and are usually faster than list as it cannot change dynamically.

It is defined within parentheses () where items are separated by commas.

```
>>> t = (5,'program', 1+3j)
```
We can use the slicing operator [] to extract items but we cannot change its value.

String is sequence of Unicode characters. We can use single quotes or double quotes to represent strings. Multi-line strings can be denoted using triple quotes, '''' or """".

```
>>> s = "This is a string"
>>> s = '''a multiline
```

Like list and tuple, slicing operator [ ] can be used with string. Strings are immutable.

PYTHON SET

Set is an unordered collection of unique items. Set is defined by values separated by comma inside braces { }. Items in a set are not ordered.

We can perform set operations like union, intersection on two sets. Set have unique values. They eliminate duplicates.

```
>>> a = {1,2,2,3,3,3}
>>> a
{1, 2, 3}
```

Since, set are unordered collection, indexing has no meaning. Hence the slicing operator [] does not work.

```
>>> a = {1,2,3}
>>> a[1]
```

Traceback (most recent call last):
   File "<string>", line 301, in runcode
   File "<interactive input>", line 1, in <module>
TypeError: 'set' object does not support indexing

PYTHON DICTIONARY

Dictionary is an unordered collection of key-value pairs.

It is generally used when we have a huge amount of data. Dictionaries are optimized for retrieving data. We must know the key to retrieve the value.

In Python, dictionaries are defined within braces {} with each item being a pair in the form key:value. Key and value can be of any type.

```
>>> d = {1:'value','key':2}
>>> type(d)
<class 'dict'>
```

CONVERSION BETWEEN DATA TYPES

We can convert between different data types by using different type conversion functions like int(), float(), str() etc.

```
>>> float(5)
5.0
```

Conversion from float to int will truncate the value (make it closer to zero).

```
>>> int(10.6)
10
>>> int(-10.6)
-10
```

Conversion to and from string must contain compatible values.

```
>>> float('2.5')
2.5
>>> str(25)
'25'
>>> int('1p')
Traceback (most recent call last):
    File "<string>", line 301, in runcode
    File "<interactive input>", line 1, in <module>
ValueError: invalid literal for int() with base 10: '1p'
```

We can even convert one sequence to another.

```
>>> set([1,2,3])
{1, 2, 3}
>>> tuple({5,6,7})
(5, 6, 7)
>>> list('hello')
['h', 'e', 'l', 'l', 'o']
```

To convert to dictionary, each element must be a pair

```
>>> dict([[1,2],[3,4]])
{1: 2, 3: 4}
>>> dict([(3,26),(4,44)])
{3: 26, 4: 44}
```

We use key to retrieve the respective value. But not the other way around.

PYTHON INPUT, OUTPUT AND IMPORT

This part focuses on two built-in functions print() and input() to perform I/O task in Python. Also, you will learn to import modules and use them in your program.

Python provides numerous built-in functions that are readily available to us at the Python prompt.

Some of the functions like input() and print() are widely used for standard input and output operations respectively. Let us see the output section first.

Python Output Using print() function

We use the print() function to output data to the standard output device (screen).

In the second print() statement, we can notice that a space was added between the string and the value of variable a.This is by default, but we can change it.

The actual syntax of the print() function is

print(*objects, sep=' ', end='\n', file=sys.stdout, flush=False)
Here, objects is the value(s) to be printed.

The sep separator is used between the values. It defaults into a space character.

After all values are printed, end is printed. It defaults into a new line.

The file is the object where the values are printed and its default value is sys.stdout (screen). Here are an example to illustrate this.

OUTPUT FORMATTING

Sometimes we would like to format our output to make it look attractive. This can be done by using the str.format() method. This method is visible to any string object.

```
>>> x = 5; y = 10
>>> print('The value of x is {} and y is {}'.format(x,y))
The value of x is 5 and y is 10
```

Here the curly braces {} are used as placeholders. We can specify the order in which it is printed by using numbers (tuple index).

We can even use keyword arguments to format the string.

```
>>> print('Hello {name}, {greeting}'.format(greeting = 'Goodmorning', name = 'John'))
Hello John, Goodmorning
```

We can even format strings like the old sprintf() style used in C programming language. We use the % operator to accomplish this.

```
>>> x = 12.3456789
>>> print('The value of x is %3.2f' %x)
The value of x is 12.35
>>> print('The value of x is %3.4f' %x)
The value of x is 12.3457
```

PYTHON INPUT

Up till now, our programs were static. The value of variables were defined or hard coded into the source code.

To allow flexibility we might want to take the input from the user. In Python, we have the input() function to allow this. The syntax for input() is

input([prompt])
where prompt is the string we wish to display on the screen. It is optional.

```
>>> num = input('Enter a number: ')
Enter a number: 10
>>> num
'10'
```

Here, we can see that the entered value 10 is a string, not a number. To convert this into a number we can use int() or float() functions.

```
>>> int('10')
10
>>> float('10')
10.0
```

This same operation can be performed using the eval() function. But it takes it further. It can evaluate even expressions, provided the input is a string

```
>>> int('2+3')
Traceback (most recent call last):
  File "<string>", line 301, in runcode
  File "<interactive input>", line 1, in <module>
ValueError: invalid literal for int() with base 10: '2+3'
>>> eval('2+3')
5
```

PYTHON IMPORT

When our program grows bigger, it is a good idea to break it into different modules.

A module is a file containing Python definitions and statements. Python modules have a filename and end with the extension .py.

Definitions inside a module can be imported to another module or the interactive interpreter in Python. We use the import keyword to do this.

For example, we can import the math module by typing in import math.

Now all the definitions inside math module are available in our scope. We can also import some specific attributes and functions only, using the from keyword. For example:

```
>>> from math import pi
>>> pi
3.141592653589793
```

While importing a module, Python looks at several places defined in sys.path. It is a list of directory locations.

```
>>> import sys
>>> sys.path
[',
 'C:\\Python33\\Lib\\idlelib',
 'C:\\Windows\\system32\\python33.zip',
 'C:\\Python33\\DLLs',
 'C:\\Python33\\lib',
 'C:\\Python33',
 'C:\\Python33\\lib\\site-packages']
```

PYTHON IF...ELSE STATEMENT

I n this part of the book, you will learn to create decisions in a Python program using different forms of if..else statement.

Decision making is required when we want to execute a code only if a certain condition is satisfied.

The if... elif... else statement is used in Python for decision making.

Python if Statement Syntax
if test expression:
    statement(s)

Here, the program evaluates the test expression and will execute statement(s) only if the text expression is True.

If the text expression is False, the statement(s) is not executed.

In Python, the body of the if statement is indicated by the indentation. Body starts with an indentation and the first unindented line marks the end.

Python interprets non-zero values as True. None and 0 are interpreted as False.

Python if Statement Flowchart

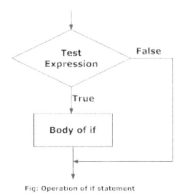

Fig: Operation of if statement

Example of if statement

```
# If the number is positive, we print an appropriate message
num = 3
if num > 0:
        print(num, "is a positive number.")
print("This is always printed.")


num = -1
if num > 0:
print("This is also always printed.")
```

Output

3 is a positive number
This is always printed
This is also always printed.

In the above example, num > 0 is the test expression.

The body of if is executed only if this evaluates to True.

When variable num is equal to 3, test expression is true and body inside body of if is executed.

If variable num is equal to -1, test expression is false and body inside body of if is skipped.

The print() statement falls outside of the if block (unindented). Hence, it is executed regardless of the test expression.

Python if...else Statement

Syntax of if...else

if test expression:

    Body of if
else:
    Body of else

The if..else statement evaluates test expression and will execute body of if only when test condition is True.

If the condition is False, body of else is executed. Indentation is used to separate the blocks.

Python if..else Flowchart

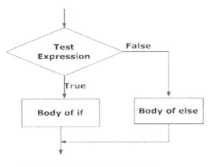

Fig: Operation of if...else statement

Example of if...else

Program checks if the number is positive or negative

And displays an appropriate message

```
num
num = 3
# Try these two variations as well.
# num = -5
# num = 0
if num >= 0:
        print("Positive or Zero")
else:
        print("Negative number")
```

In the above example, when num is equal to 3, the test expression is true and body of if is executed and body of else is skipped.

If num is equal to -5, the test expression is false and body of else is executed and body of if is skipped.

If num is equal to 0, the test expression is true and body of if is executed and body of else is skipped.

Python if...elif...else
Syntax of if...elif...else
```
if test expression:
    Body of if
elif test expression:
    Body of elif
else:
    Body of else
```

The elif is short for else if.It allows us to check for multiple expressions.

If the condition for if is False, it checks the condition of the next elif block and so on.

If all the conditions are False, body of else is executed.

Only one block among the several if...elif...else blocks is executed according to the condition.

The if block can have only one else block. But it can have multiple elif blocks.

Flowchart of if...elif...else

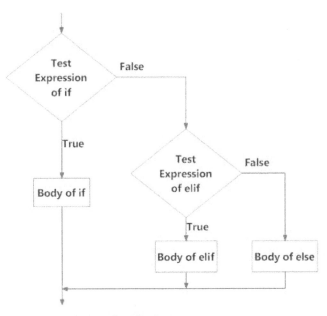

Fig: Operation of if...elif...else statement

Example of if...elif...else

In this program,

we check if the number is positive or

negative or zero and

display an appropriate message

num = 3.4

Try these two variations as well:

num = 0

num = -4.5

if num > 0:

print("Positive number")

elif num == 0:

print("Zero")

else:

print("Negative number")

When variable num is positive, Positive number is printed.

If num is equal to 0, Zero is printed.

If num is negative, Negative number is printed

PYTHON NESTED IF STATEMENTS

We can have a if...elif...else statement inside another if...elif...else statement. This is called nesting in computer programming.

Any number of these statements can be nested inside one another. Indentation is the only way to figure out the level of nesting. This can get confusing, so must be avoided if we can.

Python Nested if Example

In this program, we input a number

check if the number is positive or
negative or zero and display
an appropriate message
This time we use nested if

```
num = float(input("Enter a number: "))
if num >= 0:
    if num == 0:
        print("Zero")
    else:
        print("Positive number")
else:
    print("Negative number")
```

Output 1

Enter a number: 5
Positive num.ber

Output 2

Enter a number: -1
Negative number

Output 3

Enter a number: 0
Zero

IMPORTANT PYTHON FRAMEWORKS OF THE FUTURE FOR DEVELOPERS

A s a dynamic, general purpose and object-oriented programming language, Python is used widely by developers across the world for building a variety of software applications. Unlike other modern programming languages, Python enables programmers to express concept with less and readable code. The users also have an option to integrate Python with other popular programming languages and tools seamlessly. But it cannot be used directly for writing different types of software.

Often Python developers have to use a variety of frameworks and tools to build high quality software applications within a shorter amount of time. The resources provided by the Python frameworks help users to reduce the time and effort required for modern applications. They also have an option to choose from a number of frameworks according to the nature and requirements of individual projects. However, it is also important for the programmers to know some of the Python frameworks that will remain popular in the longer run.

10 PYTHON FRAMEWORKS THAT WILL REMAIN POPULAR

1) KIVY

As an open source Python library, Kivy makes it easier for programmers to build multi-touch user interfaces. It supports a number of popular platforms including Windows, Linux, OS X, iOS and Android. So the cross-platform framework enables users to create the app for multiple platforms using the same code base. It is also designed with features to take advantage of the native inputs, protocols and devices. Kivy further includes a fast graphic engine, while allowing users to choose from more than 20 extensible widgets.

2) QT

The open source Python framework is written in C++. Qt enables developers to build connected applications and UIs that run on multiple operating systems and devices. The developers can further create cross-platform applications and UIs without making any changes to the code. Qt further scores over other frameworks due to its comprehensive library of APIs and tools. The programmers have option to use Qt either under the community license or the commercial license.

3) PYGUI

PyGUI is considered to be simpler than other Python frameworks. But it enables developers to create GUI API by taking advantage of the language features of Python. PyGUI currently supports Windows, OS X and Linux. So the developers can use it for creating lightweight GUI APIs that can be implemented on these three platforms. They can further document the API comprehensively without referring to the documentation of any third-party GUI library.

4) WXPYTHON

The GUI toolkit for Python helps programmers to create applications with highly functional graphical user interfaces. As wxPython supports Windows, Linux and OS X, it becomes easier for developers to run the same program in multiple platforms without modifying the code. The users can write the programs in Python, while taking advantage of the 2D path drawing engine, standard dialogs, dockable windows and other features provided by the framework.

5) DJANGO

Django is the most popular high-level web application development framework for Python. Despite being open source, Django provides a simple and rapid development environment for building a variety of websites and web applications rapidly. It further helps programmers to create web application without writing lengthy code. It further comes with features to prevent some of the common security mistakes made by the developers.

6) CHERRYPY

As a minimalist web framework, CherryPy enables programs to create websites and web applications just like writing other object-oriented Python programs. So it becomes easier for developers to build web applications without writing lengthy code. CherryPy further comes with a clean interface, while allowing developers to decide the right frontend utilities and data storage option. Despite being the oldest Python web application development framework in the market, CherryPy is still being used by programmers to create a variety of modern websites.

7) FLASK

Flask is one of the micro web frameworks available for Python. Its core is simple and easy to use, but highly extensible. It also lacks many features provided by other web frameworks including database abstraction layer and form validations. Also, it does not allow users to add common functionality to the web application through third-party libraries. However, Flask enables programmers to create website rapidly by using extensions and code snippets. The snippets and patterns contributed by other members help developers to accomplish common tasks like database access, caching, file upload and authentication without writing any additional code.

8) PYRAMID

Despite being a lightweight and simple Python web framework, Pyramid is hugely popular among programmers due to its high and rapid performance. The open source framework can be used for creating a variety of applications. Once the standard Python development environment is set up, the developers can use Pyramid to build the applications rapidly. Pyramid further allows users to take advantage of an independent Model-view-controller (MVC) structure. At the same time, they can further take advantage of other frameworks by integrating them with Pyramid.

9) WEB.PY

As a simple but powerful web framework for Python, web.py helps programmers to build a variety of modern web applications rapidly. The combination of simple architecture and impressive development potential further helps users to overcome some of the common restrictions and inconveniences in web development. It still lacks many features provided by other modern web frameworks. But developers can easily integrate web.py with other frameworks to avail a number of advanced features and functionality.

10) TURBOGEARS

As a highly-scalable web application development framework for Python, TurboGears helps users to eliminate restrictions and limitations within the development environment. It can be used as a micro-framework or full-stack framework. It further provides a flexible object relationship mapper (ORM), along with supporting several databases, multiple data exchange formats, and horizontal data partitioning. The developers can further use the new widget system provided by TurboGears to effectuate development of AJAX-heavy web applications.

On the whole, the Python developers have option to choose from many frameworks. Some of these frameworks effectuate development of GUI desktop applications, whereas others help programmers to build modern websites and web application rapidly. At the same time, the developers also have option to use certain frameworks to write mobile apps in Python. That is why; it becomes essential for the developer to assess the suitability of each framework for his project based on its features and functionality. The user can also consider integrating the framework with other frameworks and tools to avail more advanced features and functionality.

PYTHON FUNCTIONS

I n this part, you'll learn about functions; what is a function, the syntax, components and types of a function. Also, you'll learn to create a function in Python.

In Python, function is a group of related statements that perform a specific task.

Functions help break our program into smaller and modular chunks. As our program grows larger and larger, functions make it more organized and manageable.

Furthermore, it avoids repetition and makes code reusable.

SYNTAX OF FUNCTION

```
def function_name(parameters):
    """docstring"""
    statement(s)
```

Above shown is a function definition which consists of following components.

1. Keyword def marks the start of function header.

2. A function name to uniquely identify it. Function naming follows the same rules of writing identifiers in Python.

3. Parameters (arguments) through which we pass values to a function. They are optional.

4. A colon (:) to mark the end of function header.

5. Optional documentation string (docstring) to describe what the function does.

6. One or more valid python statements that make up the function body. Statements must have same indentation level (usually 4 spaces).

7. An optional return statement to return a value from the function.

Example of a function

```
def greet(name):
 """This function greets to
the person passed in as
parameter"""
print("Hello, " + name + ". Good
morning!")
```

FUNCTION CALL

Once we have defined a function, we can call it from another function, program or even the Python prompt. To call a function we simply type the function name with appropriate parameters.

Try running the following into the Python shell to see the output.

```
>>> greet('Paul')
Hello, Paul. Good morning!
```

DOCSTRING

The first string after the function header is called the docstring and is short for documentation string. It is used to explain in brief, what a function does.

Although optional, documentation is a good programming practice. Unless you can remember what you had for dinner last week, always document your code.

In the above example, we have a docstring immediately below the function header. We generally use triple quotes so that docstring can extend up to multiple lines. This string is available to us as __doc__ attribute of the function.

For example:

Try running the following into the Python shell to see the output.

```
>>> print(greet.__doc__)
This function greets to
 the person passed into the
 name parameter
```

THE RETURN STATEMENT

The return statement is used to exit a function and go back to the place from where it was called.

```
Syntax of return
return [expression_list]
```
This statement can contain expression which gets evaluated and the value is returned. If there is no expression in the statement or the return statement itself is not present inside a function, then the function will return the None object.

For example:

```
>>> print(greet("May"))
Hello, May. Good morning!
None
```

Here, None is the returned value.

Example of return

```
def absolute_value(num):
    """This function returns the absolute
    value of the entered number"""
    if num >= 0:
        return num
    else:
        return -num


# Output: 2

print(absolute_value(2))


# Output: 4

print(absolute_value(-4))
```

HOW FUNCTION WORKS IN PYTHON?

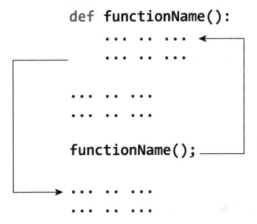

SCOPE AND LIFETIME OF VARIABLES

Scope of a variable is the portion of a program where the variable is recognized. Parameters and variables defined inside a function is not visible from outside. Hence, they have a local scope.

Lifetime of a variable is the period throughout which the variable exits in the memory. The lifetime of variables inside a function is as long as the function executes.

They are destroyed once we return from the function. Hence, a function does not remember the value of a variable from its previous calls.

Here is an example to illustrate the scope of a variable inside a function.

```
def my_func():
x = 10
print("Value inside function:",x)


x = 20


my_func()
print("Value outside function:",x)
```

Output

Value inside function: 10
Value outside function: 20

Here, we can see that the value of x is 20 initially. Even though the function my_ func() changed the value of x to 10, it did not effect the value outside the function.

This is because the variable x inside the function is different (local to the function) from the one outside. Although they have same names, they are two different variables with different scope.

On the other hand, variables outside of the function are visible from inside. They have a global scope.

We can read these values from inside the function but cannot change (write) them. In order to modify the value of variables outside the function, they must be declared as global variables using the keyword global.

TYPES OF FUNCTIONS

Basically, we can divide functions into the following two types:

1. Built-in functions - Functions that are built into Python.

2. User-defined functions - Functions defined by the users themselves.

PYTHON OBJECTS AND CLASS

I n this section, you'll learn about the core functionality of Python, Python objects and classes. You'll learn what a class is, how to create it and use it in your program.

Python is an object oriented programming language. Unlike procedure oriented programming, where the main emphasis is on functions, object oriented programming stress on objects.

Object is simply a collection of data (variables) and methods (functions) that act on those data. And, class is a blueprint for the object.

We can think of class as a sketch (prototype) of a house. It contains all the details about the floors, doors, windows etc. Based on these descriptions we build the house. House is the object.

As, many houses can be made from a description, we can create many objects from a class. An object is also called an instance of a class and the process of creating this object is called instantiation.

DEFINING A CLASS IN PYTHON

Like function definitions begin with the keyword def, in Python, we define a class using the keyword class.

The first string is called docstring and has a brief description about the class. Although not mandatory, this is recommended.

Here is a simple class definition.

```
class MyNewClass:
    '''This is a docstring. I have created a new class'''
    pass
```

A class creates a new local namespace where all its attributes are defined. Attributes may be data or functions.

There are also special attributes in it that begins with double underscores (__). For example, __doc__ gives us the docstring of that class.

As soon as we define a class, a new class object is created with the same name. This class object allows us to access the different attributes as well as to instantiate new objects of that class.

```
class MyClass:
"This is my second class"
a = 10
def func(self):

print('Hello')

# Output:
10
print(MyClass.a)

# Output: <function MyClass.func at 0x0000000003079BF8>

print(MyClass.func)
# Output: 'This is my second class'
```

CREATING AN OBJECT IN PYTHON

We saw that the class object could be used to access different attributes.

It can also be used to create new object instances (instantiation) of that class. The procedure to create an object is similar to a function call.

```
>>> ob = MyClass()
```
This will create a new instance object named ob. We can access attributes of objects using the object name prefix.

Attributes may be data or method. Method of an object are corresponding functions of that class. Any function object that is a class attribute defines a method for objects of that class.

This means to say, since MyClass.func is a function object (attribute of class), ob.func will be a method object.

```
class MyClass:
"This is my second class"

a = 10

def func(self):

print('Hello')

# create a new MyClass

ob = MyClass()

# Output: <function MyClass.func at 0x000000000335B0D0>
```

print(MyClass.func)

Output: <bound method MyClass.func of <__main__.MyClass object at 0x000000000332DEF0>>

print(ob.func)

You may have noticed the self parameter in function definition inside the class but, we called the method simply as ob.func() without any arguments. It still worked.

This is because, whenever an object calls its method, the object itself is passed as the first argument. So, ob.func() translates into MyClass.func(ob).

In general, calling a method with a list of n arguments is equivalent to calling the corresponding function with an argument list that is created by inserting the method's object before the first argument.

For these reasons, the first argument of the function in class must be the object itself. This is conventionally called self. It can be named otherwise but we highly recommend to follow the convention.

Now you must be familiar with class object, instance object, function object, method object and their differences.

CONSTRUCTORS IN PYTHON

Class functions that begins with double underscore (__) are called special functions as they have special meaning.

Of one particular interest is the __init__() function. This special function gets called whenever a new object of that class is instantiated.

This type of function is also called constructors in Object Oriented Programming (OOP). We normally use it to initialize all the variables.

```python
class ComplexNumber:

    def __init__(self,r = 0,i = 0):

        self.real = r

        self.imag = i

    def getData(self):

        print("{0}+{1}j".format(self.real,self.imag))

# Create a new ComplexNumber object

c1 = ComplexNumber(2,3)

# Call getData() function

# Output: 2+3j

c1.getData()

# Create another ComplexNumber object

# and create a new attribute 'attr'

c2 = ComplexNumber(5)

c2.attr = 10
```

```
# Output: (5, 0, 10)

print(((c2.real, c2.imag, c2.attr)))

# but c1 object doesn't have attribute 'attr'
# AttributeError: 'ComplexNumber' object has no attribute 'attr'

c1.attr
```

In the above example, we define a new class to represent complex numbers. It has two functions, __init__() to initialize the variables (defaults to zero) and getData() to display the number properly.

An interesting thing to note in the above step is that attributes of an object can be created on the fly. We created a new attribute attr for object c2 and we read it as well. But this did not create that attribute for object c1.

DELETING ATTRIBUTES AND OBJECTS

Any attribute of an object can be deleted anytime, using the del statement. Try the following on the Python shell to see the output.

```
>>> c1 = ComplexNumber(2,3)
>>> del c1.imag

>>> c1.getData()
Traceback (most recent call last):

...

AttributeError: 'ComplexNumber' object has no attribute 'imag'

>>> del ComplexNumber.getData
>>> c1.getData()
```

Traceback (most recent call last):

...

AttributeError: 'ComplexNumber' object has no attribute 'getData'

We can even delete the object itself, using the del statement.

```
>>> c1 = ComplexNumber(1,3)
>>> del c1
>>> c1
```
Traceback (most recent call last):

...

NameError: name 'c1' is not defined

Actually, it is more complicated than that. When we do c1 = ComplexNumber(1,3), a new instance object is created in memory and the name c1 binds with it.

On the command del c1, this binding is removed and the name c1 is deleted from the corresponding namespace. The object however continues to exist in memory and if no other name is bound to it, it is later automatically destroyed.

This automatic destruction of unreferenced objects in Python is also called garbage collection.

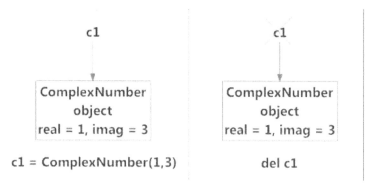

PYTHON INHERITANCE

Inheritance enable us to define a class that takes all the functionality from parent class and allows us to add more. In this article, you will learn to use inheritance in Python.

Inheritance is a powerful feature in object oriented programming.

It refers to defining a new class with little or no modification to an existing class. The new class is called derived (or child) class and the one from which it inherits is called the base (or parent) class.

Derived class inherits features from the base class, adding new features to it. This results into re-usability of code.

Python Inheritance Syntax
class DerivedClass(BaseClass):
    body_of_derived_class
Example of Inheritance in Python
To demonstrate the use of inheritance, let us take an example.

A polygon is a closed figure with 3 or more sides. Say, we have a class called Polygon defined as follows.

class Polygon:
    def __init__(self, no_of_sides):
        self.n = no_of_sides
        self.sides = [0 for i in range(no_of_sides)]

```
def inputSides(self):
    self.sides = [float(input("Enter side "+str(i+1)+" : ")) for i in range(self.n)]

    def dispSides(self):
        for i in range(self.n):
            print("Side",i+1,"is",self.sides[i])
```

This class has data attributes to store the number of sides, n and magnitude of each side as a list, sides.

Method inputSides() takes in magnitude of each side and similarly, dispSides() will display these properly.

A triangle is a polygon with 3 sides. So, we can created a class called Triangle which inherits from Polygon. This makes all the attributes available in class Polygon readily available in Triangle. We don't need to define them again (code re-usability). Triangle is defined as follows.

```
class Triangle(Polygon):
    def __init__(self):
        Polygon.__init__(self,3)

    def findArea(self):
        a, b, c = self.sides
        # calculate the semi-perimeter
        s = (a + b + c) / 2
        area = (s*(s-a)*(s-b)*(s-c)) ** 0.5
        print('The area of the triangle is %0.2f' %area)
```

However, class Triangle has a new method findArea() to find and print the area of the triangle. Here is a sample run.

```
>>> t = Triangle()
```

```
>>> t.inputSides()
Enter side 1 : 3
Enter side 2 : 5
Enter side 3 : 4

>>> t.dispSides()
Side 1 is 3.0
Side 2 is 5.0
Side 3 is 4.0

>>> t.findArea()
```

The area of the triangle is 6.00

We can see that, even though we did not define methods like inputSides() or dispSides() for class Triangle, we were able to use them.

If an attribute is not found in the class, search continues to the base class. This repeats recursively, if the base class is itself derived from other classes.

METHOD OVERRIDING IN PYTHON

In the above example, notice that __init__() method was defined in both classes, Triangle as well Polygon. When this happens, the method in the derived class overrides that in the base class. This is to say, __init__() in Triangle gets preference over the same in Polygon.

Generally when overriding a base method, we tend to extend the definition rather than simply replace it. The same is being done by calling the method in base class from the one in derived class (calling Polygon.__init__() from __init__() in Triangle).

A better option would be to use the built-in function super(). So, super().___ init(3) is equivalent to Polygon.___init___(self,3) and is preferred. You can learn more about the super() function in Python.

Two built-in functions isinstance() and issubclass() are used to check inheritances. Function isinstance() returns True if the object is an instance of the class or other classes derived from it. Each and every class in Python inherits from the base class object.

```
>>> isinstance(t,Triangle)
True
```

```
>>> isinstance(t,Polygon)
True
```

```
>>> isinstance(t,int)
False
```

```
>>> isinstance(t,object)
True
```

Similarly, issubclass() is used to check for class inheritance.

```
>>> issubclass(Polygon,Triangle)
False
```

```
>>> issubclass(Triangle,Polygon)
True
```

```
>>> issubclass(bool,int)
True
```

CONCLUSION

Python is a terrific language. The syntax is simple and code length is short which makes is easy to understand and write.

If you are getting started in programming, Python is an awesome choice. You will be amazed how much you can do in Python once you know the basics.

Python provides aspiring programmers a solid foundation based on which they can branch out to different fields. Python programming training ensures that students are able to use this highly potential programming language to the best of its capabilities in an exciting and fun way. Those who are keen to make a great career as software programmers are definite to find Python live up to their expectations.

It's easy to overlook the fact that Python is a powerful language. Not only is it good for learning programming, it's also a good language to have in your arsenal. Change your idea into a prototype or create games or get started with data Science, Python can help you in everything to get started.

Thanks for reading

© **Steven Giles**

www.ingramcontent.com/pod-product-compliance
Lightning Source LLC
Chambersburg PA
CBHW071030050326
40689CB00014B/3591